More Comments about The LinkedIn Personal Trainer:

"What Steve Tylock says makes sense. Follow his straight forward approach to creating your LinkedIn profile with information that lets companies, recruiters, colleagues and business contacts find you quickly. Link up with people you know and trust and your connections will help you reach your goals!"

Lynn Dessert, President, Leadership Breakthrough, Inc. and Blog Author, Elephants at Work.

"I give seminars on LinkedIn to job seekers, execs in transitions, sales reps and entrepreneurs. LinkedIn is a valuable business tool and provides very useful functionality for each of those communities. In the spirit of the 'for dummies' series, Steve takes a complex site, which itself doesn't provide more than rudimentary help files, and presents the material in bite-sized, easily digestible chunks for the novice user. I would recommend it for anyone who has decided to use LinkedIn and wants to do it right from the very beginning."

Ed Callahan, Partner and Co-Founder, Momentum Technology Partners.

"You've heard of the tremendous benefits of using LinkedIn, and decided to give it a try. After joining and creating a profile – you wait for results. OR you can benefit from having Steve Tylock at your side as your "personal trainer" to help you maximize your success by creating a compelling profile that achieves results. For a fraction of the cost of one session with a personal trainer, save yourself hours of learning spread over many months, by using this book with its tips, suggestions, and exercises as you work at the computer. This book will pay off many times your financial and time investment."

Molly Kidwell, International Solutions Manager.

The Revised LinkedIn Personal Trainer

Using LinkedIn to find, get found, and network your way to success

Steven Tylock

Tylock and Company, LLC

Rochester, New York

Notice of Liability

While great efforts have been taken to ensure the accuracy of the information contained in this book, the contents are presented "as is", without warranty.

Trademarks and Cover Art

LinkedIn is a trademark of the LinkedIn Corporation

Front and back cover artwork publicly available from NASA and Visible Earth at: http://visibleearth.nasa.gov/ & http://www.nasa.gov/

First Edition 2007
Second Edition 2011, revised

ISBN-13: 978-1466269439

Table of Contents

Foreword to the Revised Edition

As I was considering Steve's revision of his book, it occurred to me that I had joined LinkedIn fairly early in its inception. I checked the date - 6 years ago.

The reason I joined LinkedIn in those early days is because I wanted to know about and eventually meet my professional counterparts in other parts of the country. At first there weren't many contacts, but membership grew over time. As the network became larger and larger, I proselytized about the system to my corporate colleagues. Alas, they didn't see the value at first. But over the years they came around and now virtually all have joined.

Steve's book is a gentle reminder of the advantages of joining LinkedIn, which are now many times more than what they were. I use the system every single day. In my work as a management consultant and executive coach, LinkedIn is the single best tool to meet people, assess talent, and make connections for myself and on behalf of my clients.

There are so many uses for LinkedIn, that they would fill several pages of this Foreword. Suffice it to say that once you've developed a good profile and connection list, you can make significant strides in advocating for yourself and others. Steve's book will help you create a better profile, and establish your professional connections sooner.

Let Steve take you on a concise and insightful tour of the power of LinkedIn.

Luis Martinez
Strategic HR consultant, Executive coach, Author, Speaker.

Foreword to the Original Edition

LinkedIn is a powerful business networking platform used by over 10 Million members.

But the question is: are members getting enough out of LinkedIn to see just how much this powerful platform can help them, their businesses, and their social causes?

As the founder of MyLinkedInPowerForum.com and many other LinkedIn-centric discussion groups, I've had the pleasure of talking with many professionals from all around the world about why LinkedIn is such a great business tool.

Thus, I'm truly happy that Steven Tylock has patiently written a wonderful book that can help even the newest LinkedIn user get immediate benefits from the power within LinkedIn.

What I personally like about LinkedIn Personal Trainer is what is too often left out of books on professional networking: exercises.

Exercises help us get a feel for the things we learn - much as learning to ride a bicycle is accomplished by practice, not just instruction.

Readers who complete the exercises in LinkedIn Personal Trainer will be able to confidently use LinkedIn to address their business and career objectives. And what's more, LinkedIn Personal Trainer makes an excellent gift for friends, family members, and business associates who can use the power of LinkedIn to help them, too.

Vincent Wright
Founder MyLinkedInPowerForum

Acknowledgements

I'd like to thank my wife and family for letting me do my thing to create this book, John for working with me on all of my different projects, and Kathleen for suggesting I develop this material.

Introduction

LinkedIn can help you find, and get found by more than 120 million members. Some of those members have spent considerable time building their profile and connection network – and get a great payback for those efforts.

Individuals at the other end of the spectrum accepted an initial invitation to begin using the service, created a profile with the most rudimentary of information, and are waiting to see the benefit.

The material in this book creates a "personal training" session that will help move you from an inexperienced user of LinkedIn to one who finds, gets found, and networks efficiently.

LinkedIn helps you network but does not network for you

Your use of LinkedIn will not magically bring you in contact with special people, but it will help build your network, organize your connections, and help you find (and reach) people you might never otherwise know of.

Results are proportional to effort

I have talked with light users of the system who don't see a return in value. When I turn the situation around and ask how much time and effort they have devoted, they see why - they haven't put any effort into the game.

If you're looking for a frog,

spend some time near a pond…

This book offers advice and training exercises

I developed this material working one on one with individual users who grew from a basic understanding of LinkedIn to become fully functional users.

Each section includes a thought provoking question, advice, and an exercise – helping you understand why you want to take specific actions. Your profile is just that – yours, and your unique situation means that there are no stock answers. By understanding the intent of each feature, you will be in the best position to use it effectively.

As you complete each section's exercise, you will move yourself closer to your LinkedIn goals – finding, being found, and networking productively.

This material was originally part of a ninety-minute private training session – the student was not expected to complete his or her changes in that time, but could finish the exercises later. You may want to read through once and provide short answers to the exercises - returning later to fill in more and expand on your initial answers.

Tip – open a web browser to your account and follow along.

What effect will weak connections have on your ability to use the LinkedIn network?

Connections – strong ties between individuals

The first and most significant concept in LinkedIn is that of connections. Without connections (and everything that relates to them), the system would be just another "here I am" sort of site.

With the concept of connections, everything changes. Connections represent trusted relationships. Relationships that help build businesses:

- Current and past co-workers
- Respected clients and partners
- Trusted suppliers and vendors
- Members of professional associations

The distinction being that not every relationship you have ever had is worthy of being a connection. Would you refer a trusted partner to one of your former co-workers who did an unacceptable or merely adequate job? Of course not!

And so, as a network of trusted connections, your obligation is to include quality relationships. Relationships with individuals you would gladly introduce to others in your network - without hesitation.

You will find some LinkedIn users who believe that anyone met via one email is worthy of becoming a trusted connection. There are some specific advantages and disadvantages to this approach; my view is that the disadvantages outweigh the advantages. See Appendix A for more on this.

Action: Identify several individuals whom you trust:

_____

_____

_____

How often will you be found with an

empty profile?

Profile – a rich description of an individual

Not just any profile – *your profile!* This is the one place where you have complete control over how you are presented to the LinkedIn public.

While not a résumé, you want to include much of what is often put into a résumé:

- Summary of your professional history
- Specialties
- Current position
- Highlights from your career
- Significant volunteer activities
- Publications
- Education
- Special activities

By including a rich description of your skills, interests, and positions - both current and past, you increase the likelihood that others will find you!

Provide information that gives someone a good reason to talk to you. (And isn't it more enjoyable to talk to someone who is interesting and active?)

Action: Note interesting portions of your background. Include activities where you work with others:

_____

_____

_____

_____

What happens when you send people a note and they <u>don't</u> see your message, but you think they have?

The LinkedIn "Home"

The *Home* tab is the starting point when you log in to LinkedIn. It provides a summary of the activities of your connections, suggests a few things, and lets you update your connections on your activities.

Inbox

The inbox now has its own tab, but that doesn't change how it works. It holds requests – Introductions, Invitations, and other items. (In general, you will want these to be sent to your regular email address, but in case your email is lost, you can find them all here) Should you attempt to invite someone and the email address is incorrect (they no longer have that address, or you mistyped it), you will find a returned message here.

Inside the Inbox are folders for general Messages and Invitations. In addition LinkedIn provides folders for Sent, Archived and Trash.

LinkedIn's email-like messaging isn't very powerful or nearly as useful as your regular email account. You probably want to send messages to people over regular email once you've made contact through LinkedIn.

Action: Take action on items in your Inbox. Do you need to follow up with any of those contacts to move things along?

_____

_____

_____

_____

_____

What kinds of people will be receptive

when you reach out?

Updates

Who in your network is updating their activities, adding connections, changing their profiles, and hiring?

It is nice to see which of your contacts are "growing" their network. The system tells you who has been adding connections recently. (The term "connection" probably doesn't mean much right now, but hang on, we'll cover this whole topic a bit later in the book)

When LinkedIn users update their profiles significantly, the system will "update" the people they connect with, letting them know that something has changed.

> **Tip**: You may not want to update *your* network when you make small changes. Look in "Settings" when you mouse over your name in the upper right corner. Select "Profile – Privacy Controls" to turn off your activity broadcasts.

Remember - LinkedIn is also telling your connections about your activity. Who are you connecting to? What changes have you made to your profile lately? What updates have you entered into the system? As you scan the updates of others, keep in mind how you can use the system to stay in front of them.

Action: Which of your current connections are actively adding connections? Could any of the people they connect to also be your connections?

_____

_____

_____

_____

_____

_____

How much larger is a network

where everyone has 30

connections instead of 20?

(It's not 50%)

(20x20x20 = 8000)

(30x30x30 = 27000)

(That's 237% larger!)

Just Joined LinkedIn and Other Blurbs

Below the updates area is a section devoted to helping you build your network. If you've worked at an organization or been to school with people, LinkedIn wants to make it easy for you to reconnect with individuals who were also there. To help, they show you who else lists that employer or school – you can review the list and reconnect to the people you recognize.

After you have completed the initial effort to add these members, the system will let you know when more people from an organization have started using LinkedIn – to let you review their names as well.

Off to the side you'll find several interesting tools that help you see what else is happening on the system. New tools may also appear.

People You May Know – LinkedIn matches patterns to guess who else you might know and suggests them as connections.

Who's Viewed Your Profile – If you're willing to let others know you've visited their profiles, you can see who's visited yours. (But only see generic details unless others have agreed to show their name)

Your LinkedIn Network – a review of your network information. Click through to see other interesting details about it.

Jobs You May Be Interested In – A preview of the jobs tab, more details in the jobs link below.

Action: Click "See more >>" in the "People You May Know" section. Do you recognize any of the names listed? Note them here to invite later.

_____

_____

_____

What do you want to be found for?

Profile

Your profile is your public face on LinkedIn. It presents your professional experiences, accomplishments, and interests. By professional, I mean those activities that drive your business, income, and relationships – as well as hobbies and passions that you believe will provide a connection to others.

When viewing the top "boxed" portion of this tab on LinkedIn, it lists information from the areas below. You can use the buttons to edit directly, or can scroll down and see those areas in more detail.

Basic Information & Summary

The first section includes *name, headline, location, & industry*. The headline is the single thing that you want to say about yourself to everyone who finds you – think about this carefully.

If you have a good quality, professional, digital image of yourself, go ahead and upload it. People like to see faces. If you don't have a good picture or are not photogenic, don't worry about it.

The summary section includes *professional experience & specialties*. This lets you describe yourself more fully and gives you a soapbox. Paint a picture of yourself and your interests. One enterprising sales professional listed his specific successes under the specialties section.

> **Tip**: When writing for LinkedIn text boxes, compose inside the word processor of your choice (in a plain font with no special formatting) and paste into the LinkedIn box – you'll be able to check spelling and sentence structure in your word processor.

Action: List the top five "key value propositions" in your current situation. Make sure they end up inside the summary section in one form or another.

Would you rather be involved with someone who has a boring history or an interesting story?

Applications & Experience

LinkedIn has added more than a dozen third party applications to offer enhanced content on your profile. It isn't something you will want to do initially. Later on when you're more comfortable, check out the options and add what seems appropriate. One aspect to keep in mind: just because you can, doesn't mean you should. Don't clutter your profile!

The Experience section follows Applications unless you move things around. I recommend the default order for items until you understand the site well and decide to customize your profile for a specific reason. I suggest you include all of the official, unofficial, and volunteer roles you have had. If the only position you list is your current one, how useful are you to others?

By listing all of the organizations you have had a significant involvement with, you can be "found" for all of them. In addition, you add the opportunity to have others recommend you for your good work together (more on that later).

You don't need your entries to look like they came from your résumé – explain in business terms what you did and what you accomplished. Give a searcher a reason to ask you about your days building the XYZ product!

> **Tip**: You don't need to mention a short term engagement that doesn't have any real significance.

Action: Identify the significant organizations you have worked for – both in the past and currently. Update your profile to include them.

How close were the bonds you

formed in school?

Are those individuals on LinkedIn?

Education

List your school(s) and degree(s). If you have extra involvement on or off campus, you can add it to one of the "notes" sections.

Perhaps you have some specialty training. This might make a great place for mentioning your "Six-Sigma" or "Project Management Professional" training.

Other training you've had may be more focused on an industry or skill. Whatever it is, your options are open.

Action: Update your LinkedIn "Education" profile.

_____

_____

_____

_____

_____

_____

_____

*Of all the great things that have ever
been said about you by great people,
can any of your new contacts
easily "see" them?*

*What would you think of a LinkedIn
member who had hundreds of connections
but no endorsements?*

Recommendations

When you are looking to begin a relationship with an individual, you like seeing that someone else has endorsed the work of the person you are considering, don't you? You're happy to let others know about the good works of people you trust, correct? Others are happy to do the same for you, right?

So let's get going!

Recommendations are a great way to establish that you are trusted and trusting. It is a step forward along the path of relationship building, and LinkedIn wants to help you do it.

You want to recommend your trusted contacts, and you want to ask for their recommendations as well. While it is often true that recommendations are reciprocal, they needn't be.

> **Tip**: You have full control over recommendations. When they are initially offered, you must approve and determine whether each is visible. Should someone submit one with a typo, or say something in an awkward way, ask them to resubmit it and offer a correction.

Action: Identify three people whom you can recommend, and three whom you can ask for recommendations:

_____

_____

_____

_____

_____

_____

Do you like to work with interesting people? Do you think others like to work with interesting people?

Additional Information

Note all of the things you are involved in that fall outside the classical boundaries of employment. Subheadings include: Websites, Twitter, Interests, Groups & Associations, and Honors & Awards.

This makes a good spot to include your civic, youth, artistic, volunteer, and otherwise fun endeavors. (Of course, if you spend enough time on something that it looks like a job, you might add it as a job above)

As an example – I am not the only person in the Rochester area who considers their involvement in Orienteering worth mentioning. While not a deal-maker, it may give me something else to talk about with a new contact.

All groups that you join on LinkedIn will be listed here unless you've chosen not to share that information. (More on this later in the Groups description)

To balance this concept, all of the material you place here (and on your profile) should support your professional image. Think hard before including material that might create a negative bias in some readers. It is possible to reveal too much information.

Action: What additional items about yourself should you mention in your profile?

_____

_____

_____

_____

_____

If someone wanted to get in touch with you to discuss a business deal, would you want that message delayed?

Contact Settings, Personal Information & Additions

What opportunities you are interested in hearing about and how you should be contacted?

LinkedIn is interested in making the "right" connections. If you don't want to hear about job offers, you shouldn't! By the same token, you should take others' settings into consideration when you contact them.

Set these as wide as you are comfortable with, and make sure that you hear about items quickly – direct email to your regular account.

Some LinkedIn users have wanted, and asked for the ability to include other personal information on their profile. In response, LinkedIn added a section to list phone, address, IM, birthday, and even marital status.

I'm not particularly eager to share any of those details at this level, but this is certainly an area of personal choice. Don't feel obliged to share any of these; you may just ignore this section.

And consider your profile's message as LinkedIn continues to evolve the site and allow the addition of certifications, languages, patents, publications, and even individual skills. It may be that the feature is of benefit to you, or it just might be a bit too much.

Action: Determine what contact types you are interested in, and set your profile accordingly.

How do you rate others when you see errors in the materials they write?

Profile Completeness & View as others see it

LinkedIn has a gauge to determine whether users have filled out their profile. This is an arbitrary meter that considers how many of the areas you have completed, and how many jobs you have entered. If it acts as an incentive to get you to keep working at building your profile, great. If it bothers you, ignore it.

The View Profile tab allows you to view your profile as other see it. Use this page to proof your layout.

You may also want to ask one of your close contacts to review your profile and give you feedback (truly seeing it as others see it). Be sure to ask someone that you trust to give you a critical review, a mere acquaintance or family member will likely say that it looks nice...

Action: View your profile and note what needs to be cleaned up.

_____

_____

_____

_____

_____

_____

_____

Is there an individual that can give you a great recommendation, but you hate to bother them all the time?

Recommendations & Profile Organizer

We've seen where recommendations fit on your profile, and the Recommendations tab allows you to manage those. Manage received ones, recommend others, manage the recommendations you have given, and ask for them.

A good goal is to have at least one recommendation for each position you list. A second is to get recommendations from bosses, peers, subordinates, and customers. Don't go overboard though; people look suspiciously at profiles with 200 of them.

Additionally, the Profile Organizer is a feature open to members that pay for an account. When you've found an interesting profile and want to keep track of it, you can save it to the profile organizer.

This might be of greater interest to a recruiter or sales person, and is one more reason to use the paid service – if you have a need.

Action: Review the "Request Recommendations" tab and see how easy it is to ask for one. Outline what you might say in your request.

_____

_____

_____

_____

_____

_____

_____

This is another place to ask yourself:

how do I want to be found?

Public Profile (Web)

LinkedIn offers a version of your profile over the web for anyone to see. The contents of that profile are completely up to you!

Reach this area with the *Edit* button next to the "Public Profile" item in the main Edit Profile area. You may claim a web page for your profile, and this is a must. The default location is not very useful.

And this web page makes a great addition to your signature! Would you rather be:

http://www.linkedin.com/pub/john-smith/12/85b/384

or

http://www.linkedin.com/in/stevetylock

Review the sections of your profile that can be made available to determine what you'd like to release.

Note: the information in your public profile *will* be indexed by Google!

Tip: Edit "Your Public Profile URL" and claim a human readable page, add that URL to your email signature.

Action: What sections of your profile do you want released to the web?

_____

_____

_____

_____

_____

If your LinkedIn profile is the best description of yourself, doesn't it make sense to call it to people's attention?

Email Signatures

LinkedIn offers the ability to build a snappy email signature. Click "Tools" at the bottom of any page and find the "Email Signatures" link. The tool includes areas for all the different types of information LinkedIn thinks people put in signatures, and allows you to specify one of several layouts.

I prefer a simple signature that can be expressed without formatting, but the great thing about it is that you are free to select according to your own preferences!

Action: Select the information you would like in your signature and use the LinkedIn email signature tool to create your new signature.

———————————————————

———————————————————

———————————————————

———————————————————

———————————————————

———————————————————

———————————————————

Have you maximized your ability to be found based on your profile?

Findability

Profiles are parsed by LinkedIn to make it easy for members to find contacts. These searches (explained in detail later) reach into your profile for key words and names.

For example, if you want to find a consultant specializing in turning around IT infrastructures, you can type "turnaround IT consultant" into the keyword search window and get results.

How do you get found for your specialty? Mention it in your profile! You can't be found for something you don't mention!

Action: Review your profile one last time to find out whether you have everything you want in there. Search for yourself using common keywords and see if your profile comes up! List additional steps you will take over the next 30 days to increase your reach:

_____

_____

_____

_____

_____

_____

_____

Do you have an easy way (outside of LinkedIn) to see what your network connections have been up to recently?

Contacts

You reach into the LinkedIn world through your contacts. You "see" three levels of information: your contacts (1), their contacts (2), and the contacts of your contacts' contacts (3). In addition, LinkedIn will let you see information about a limited number of people who are not "in" your network, but will hide the names of those people.

All of your connections have profiles and connections of their own.

The *Contacts* page lists each of your connections, their picture, and the size of their network. You may add "Tags" to your connections – these are seen only by you, and it's a great way to sort contacts into groupings. Identify those that worked at the same company, attended the same school, or have kids in your school.

Connection's Profiles

I hope your connections have taken as much time to build their profile as you have!

Their profiles will fill in information that you might not be aware of such as other positions, specialties, and interests.

Not only can you review their profiles individually, you can use the LinkedIn search tool to find individuals in your network who meet certain criteria (more on searching later).

Action: List three companies that you'd like to learn that you have a connection to:

_____

_____

_____

What's larger, connecting to 100 people who each connect to 20 more or connecting to 50 people who each connect to 50?

Connection's connections

Each of your connections has connections – their own network. By default you can see your connections' names (and they can see the names of people in your network). Your network increases when your connections add to their networks.

Help your friends grow their own networks!

> **Tip:** Should you not want to reveal the names of your connections to your other connections, you can do so under "Settings" → "Profile" → "Select who can see your connections". Be careful as this is a trust issue – telling your connections that you don't trust them to see whom you connect to is a powerful message. (I only connect to people I trust, I leave my connection list open.)

Action: Look over some of your direct connections. List some of their contacts that could become your contacts (because you already know them):

_____

_____

_____

_____

_____

_____

_____

Can you think of a situation in your environment that would lead you to want to cut off an association?

Removing connections

Sometimes you wind up with a connection that you added without realizing that you didn't know the person well, or perhaps the relationship has changed and you no longer want to list them. LinkedIn provides a mechanism to remove connections, and that silently severs the relationship.

Action: Find the "Remove Connections" dialogue in the upper right corner of the "Contacts" screen – click on it to see the screen that is used to remove connections.

_____

_____

_____

_____

_____

_____

_____

Was there any aspect of LinkedIn that you wondered about before you understood it better? Can you describe LinkedIn better so that your invitations don't get held up while the recipient checks it out?

Invitations

LinkedIn is all about inviting contact. You invite others already on the system to join your network. You also invite people who are not yet part of LinkedIn to join. Others will find you and invite you to join their network.

Once established, your network becomes a means to invite others into appropriate business discussions.

You'll find dialogue boxes to use to invite people on many of the screens. (Descriptions for the additional options *Imported Contacts* and *Colleagues & Classmates* follow this page). At the basic level, you invite with an email address, a first name, and a last name. You add a personalized message about using LinkedIn and send it off.

> **Tip**: LinkedIn will supply a sample message for your invitation. Please personalize it. (It's your personal invitation, not spam. The canned message is not very personal.)

> **Tip**: LinkedIn allows you to "mass mail" a large group of people at one time. Unless you can craft a message to the group along the lines of "I'm looking to get in touch with everyone from the Acme Development Team", you're better off sending individual invitations with a personal message.

You want to invite people to both join your network as well as join LinkedIn. The former is a bit easier. You know they use the tool and, if they remember you, the connection should follow. If they do not use LinkedIn, you need to explain the benefits: find and get found, no cost, and safety. For your network to grow, you've got to encourage people to join your network in both ways.

Action: List groups of people you'd like to invite:

_____

_____

_____

Should you invite people to connect just because you have their email addresses?

Other Contacts & Access to LinkedIn

LinkedIn wants you to be successful – expanding your list of connections will help make you successful, and using LinkedIn in conjunction with whatever platform you like makes it easy.

LinkedIn can take the email addresses that you have in your email program and compare that list against the email-address-based user accounts it keeps.

Because of the prevalence of webmail (Yahoo, gmail, AOL, Hotmail), Microsoft Outlook, Lotus Notes, and Mobile Phones, LinkedIn has developed programs that work specifically with each. (If you use another mail reader you can export your contact list and import it via another mechanism.) You can find out who is already using LinkedIn!

Download the Outlook Toolbar, Lotus, and Mobile Apps under the "Tools" heading of the bottom menu.

For webmail and importing contact files, select "Add Connections" from the Contacts area.

The tools are great to use, but make it too easy to send a mass invitation to everyone who has ever sent you an email. Remember the rule about only inviting your trusted contacts? Just send out individual connection requests to the specific people you identify. It will take longer, but you will have a better network because of it.

Action: Use LinkedIn's tool to pull in your main email program's contact list – invite your close contacts who are already members of LinkedIn, and then write invitations for those who are not yet part of LinkedIn.

_____

_____

_____

Is it easier to establish a connection while you work with someone, or after you have left an organization?

Colleagues & Classmates

The Colleagues & Classmates sections help you re-connect with associates from former jobs and schools. Look for these within "Add Connections" under the Contacts area.

It does this by searching for members who share the company or college that you list. You will have an opportunity to re-connect to people you know.

If you list the years you were at the company or college, LinkedIn will look for others with overlapping time periods.

> **Tip**: some people will attempt to connect to "everyone" who was at the same large company – even if they didn't know the individuals. You don't want to do that.

Action: Which former colleagues would you like to re-connect with?

_____

_____

_____

_____

_____

_____

Doesn't it feel great to be invited into

someone else's network?

Receiving Invitations

In the same way that you are reaching out to find your former co-workers, classmates, colleagues, and friends, others are doing the same – and they may find you before you find them!

When you receive an invitation from someone you trust, by all means accept it. (There is one caution about having multiple email addresses and potentially creating multiple LinkedIn accounts – please make sure you read the advice on multiple email addresses found on page 71.)

> **Tip**: If you don't remember someone, reply and ask the person to remind you how you knew each other.

You will also receive invitations from people you don't know. In the same way that you should not invite anyone to join your network unless you know and trust them, you should not accept invitations from anyone you don't know and trust. (Mega-Connectors are discussed more in Appendix A.)

Action: Review any open invitations in your Inbox.

_____

_____

_____

_____

If you worked at a larger organization, you might not be willing to connect to every person there, but would you feel an affinity for other ex-employees?

Groups

LinkedIn allows users to join up to 50 groups, 50 sub-groups, and create 10 groups of your own. Others in the same group can start conversations, see each other's profiles, and safely get in touch – through LinkedIn.

You are not provided contact information for group members, and there are no mass-group contact methods, but it still provides a great way to reach others that share membership in the group.

Groups are strictly opt-in, and you should check to see if any alumni, ex-employee, or other networking organizations that you belong to have established a group.

In addition, look for groups around the topics that you're passionate about.

If the group you want to join does not already exist you can create it yourself!

When you're participating in a group discussion, take care in how you post – everyone within the group will be able to see it. You'd probably rather not have everyone think you're a hot-head or can't compose proper English sentences.

Action: Note some groups that you belong to and check to see if LinkedIn has established a group for them:

_____

_____

_____

_____

_____

Suppose there is a company that you are looking to partner with. What resources do you have to find out about the company and the people who work there?

Now you have one more.

Search (People)

The LinkedIn search menu is the mechanism to turn your effort in building a network and creating a profile into results.

The "Search" and "Advanced Search" buttons are displayed prominently in the upper right on all screens. In addition to searching for People, you can search through Updates, Jobs, Companies, Answers, Groups, and your Inbox. It's important to learn to use search and the advanced options.

Keywords, **Name**, **Title**, **Company**: Search your network for instances of words in these specific locations of a profile.

Location, **Industry**, **Interested In**, **Joined Network**: Limit the search according to any of these factors.

Tip: Select a country (US), a blank ZIP Code, and the "located in or near" item to restrict the search to anywhere in the US.

Sort by: Allows you to arrange the results according to a variety of factors. Try them out.

Search results may be refined by editing the search criteria to the left of your results. Should the results include too many members, add another condition or otherwise restrict the search.

When you select a profile from a search, you see that profile. Review and contact, if you wish! (see "Introductions" on page 63)

Action: Using the companies you wanted to find information about (from the "Connection's Profiles" Action), conduct some sample searches.

As a job searcher, how helpful is it to check into the job and poster?

As a job poster, can you see a benefit in reviewing the applicant's profile with recommendations?

Jobs

For the seeker, LinkedIn provides tools to search through job postings. For the savvy company, LinkedIn provides opportunities to post openings (for a fee).

When looking for a position, LinkedIn will search its internal database first, and then partner with Simply Hired to show positions discovered over the web.

After you've found a position posted on LinkedIn, not only will you see who posted the position, you'll have a built-in path of trusted network connections to reach them! In some instances, companies post positions without contact information – when that happens, use the search tool to find out who in your network works at the target company. Ask your trusted connection for a referral for the opening! Ask about the company and the people there!

For those with job openings to fill, you can check out your candidates! This is better than looking up information on applicants that come with just a résumé and cover letter. In addition to the online profile and recommendations, you can find other LinkedIn members who have worked with the companies noted. ("Reference Search" is enabled for paid accounts and accounts used to post jobs.)

Action: Look up several jobs that you might be interested in looking at or would be similar to positions you need to fill.

Would you like to find an overview

of your target companies?

Companies

The *Companies* tab allows organizations to create an overview message while LinkedIn consolidates demographic information about the individuals that work at the company.

When you'd like to get some background on a company, this is one place to check first. The overview is provided by the company, but all of the other data about who's at the company, recently been hired, promoted, or active is from LinkedIn. LinkedIn partners with Business Week to provide additional information about the company.

When you're marketing a company, have a look here as well. If others are reading this material, what impressions are they forming? And while you can't control the content of individual user's profiles, you might see some elements within this area that can be changed, or may prompt a suggestion.

Action: Review the company profile for your existing employer, or an employer you'd like to get hired by. Jot your notes here.

_____

_____

_____

_____

_____

_____

_____

Would you like to ask something of your network?

Would you like to answer a question from someone in your network?

Answers

LinkedIn's "Answers" section (under "More") allows members to ask and answer business related questions. It is one of the few methods available to reach out to your network and, as such, it is prone to abuse (as users learn how to get value from it).

Your question or answer is widely seen; so take care to make sure it reflects well on you.

Please don't use the section to "troll" for contact.

It can be used to recruit, advertise, or announce items - including looking for a job - but you've got to use the Jeopardy hook:

"I'm looking for work in the construction industry, what spots are currently undergoing a boom in that sector?"

(Notice how it asks a question, but also says "I'm looking"?)

This area is ignored by some users, and loved by others. Your participation is up to you and your comfort level.

Action: Click into the Answers section and see if there are any questions posed that you'd like to answer (and do so).

Do you enjoy adding extra features?

Additional Applications

LinkedIn opened up the platform to allow third parties to develop additional features through applications. You can access them through the "More" -> "Get More Applications" area.

Some are better than others, and all are worth a look.

Here are a few you probably want to try out:

- Reading List by Amazon – if you keep one there

- WordPress – if you manage a blog on this platform

- Events – who's planning what

- Polls – a bit simplistic, but fun to look at

I'm not a fan of some applications like "My Travel". Early in my career some suspicious events happened at home when I advertised that I was traveling and I no longer care to advertise such. Your mileage may vary.

Action: Look through the applications to see if there is one or more you'd like to work with. Note them here to return to.

_____

_____

_____

_____

_____

Are you more agreeable to a conversation

if one of your trusted friends

recommended the other party to you?

Reaching out through Introductions!

Outside of searching, the other significant benefit from your network is the ability to contact other LinkedIn members. You may want to discuss a new business opportunity, a partnership, a job, a reference, or a sale – the potential is limitless and entirely up to you!

The special aspect of this contact is that it is via a chain of mutual trusted connections.

Let's say that you connect to Mary, and Mary connects to John. You'd like to contact John in order to discuss a business opportunity. While you can use LinkedIn to find out about Mary's connection to John and can always pick up the phone to talk to Mary directly, LinkedIn includes a way for you to send a message to John and route it through Mary. You might type:

> "John, I'd like to get together with you to discuss a sales opportunity with the XYZ Corporation…"

And you would also include a message to Mary:

> "Mary, I'm hoping you can introduce me to John – I think we have a great business opportunity together."

Your "Get Introduced" message goes first to Mary – she sees both your message to John and to her and has the chance to approve or deny the message. Because members generally trust each other, the inclination is to make worthwhile requests and to approve them. But, if Mary does not approve the message, John never sees it.

If she approves the message, she forwards the original along with her own addition:

> "John, I've worked with Steve for several years - you'll want to make the time to talk with him."

John then sees Mary's recommendation and the original message (the message to Mary may or may not be visible depending on edits).

*Do you have better success when you
are introduced to your new clients
by your existing clients?*

[Introductions continued]

It's possible to send a message to third degree connections as well. Each person in the chain must approve and forward the request. If a request is denied, you'll get notified.

By building the communication stream through trusted connections, weak or bogus requests will not get through. (Should one of my friends get involved with a multi-level marketing system, I'm not likely to pass those requests through to my other close connections.)

When multiple connection paths reach your target, you decide which of your contacts it should start through. Send your message over a route that is 2 levels deep in preference to 3 levels, and otherwise choose your contact with the best relationship.

All basic accounts can have 5 active introduction requests. If you'd like to withdraw one, open your Inbox, select "Sent", find the words "All Messages" with a little triangle and click there, select "Introductions", and click on the specific introduction you'd like to withdraw. At the bottom of that message, you'll find a small "Withdraw" button.

Action: Plan an introduction for a LinkedIn user you want to get to know better. (Perhaps someone you found in the earlier search)

Would you feel safer if you contact people

and they can reply

but don't see your email address directly?

Messaging

LinkedIn allows several ways to contact other members.

Your contacts see your updates on their home page.

You can send messages to any of your direct contacts (up to 50 at a time). To do this, go to your "InBox" and "Compose Message".

And you can send a message to fellow group members by entering the groups area, selecting the specific group, and clicking on the "Members" tab. Find the individual you'd like to contact (perhaps with the search dialogue). When you place your cursor over their entry, "Send Message" appears to the left – select that and complete the message.

Each of these items can be used, overused, or even abused – moderation is a good thing!

In the same way that you'll contact others about changes in your life, they'll be sending you notices of their own.

Action: Plan updates so that your network will see what is happening in your career and business.

_____

_____

_____

_____

_____

_____

Compare the level of trust you would

assess for messages that come from

    a)   a trusted contact,
    b)   an InMail, or
    c)   an unsolicited email

Does InMail provide a leg up versus

an unsolicited email?

Upgrading your account and InMail

LinkedIn understands that introduction attempts three levels deep may be less likely to work out – and that they will take extra time to reach the final connection.

To help provide quick connections, they developed InMail. InMail is a feature that lets one member contact another member directly, without the use of the introduction network. This feature can also be used to contact others who are outside of their network.

For example, if you're a recruiter, this is very helpful if you're searching for people based on their profiles.

The use of InMail requires an upgraded account or purchase of one or more units of InMail. The account levels offer different monthly quantities of InMail messages, and InMails may be purchased on the Settings page.

If you don't need to contact people like this, the standard (free) account works quite well.

Configuring your account to receive all types of messages, including InMail is accomplished on the "Settings" → "Email Preferences" tab. You can decline all InMail if you prefer, and so can other members.

Action: Jot down some situations where you might like to get in touch with someone through LinkedIn with an InMail:

_____

_____

_____

_____

Do you use more than one

email address?

Multiple Email Addresses

The most common problem individuals have asked me to help fix is that of having multiple LinkedIn accounts.

An individual generally doesn't understand how it happens, but the following story illustrates it – if you remember that your email address defines your account name.

> John Smith (jsmith@somecompany.com) starts using LinkedIn, creates an initial profile with basic information, and invites a half dozen trusted contacts. Things are working well.
>
> Later that week John's good friend Sally notices that John is using LinkedIn and says "Hey, John's in now. I better invite him!"
>
> Sally thinks John has a personal email at jsmith@someISP.com and uses that when LinkedIn asks for an email address.
>
> LinkedIn knows that those two "accounts" are different and sends off a new invitation to the new John Smith.
>
> John reads the email at home and thinks "This is great! I'm adding Sally!"
>
> He doesn't realize that he is creating a new account for this new email address when he clicks on the link.
>
> Six months later someone points out that there are two John Smiths in the system and they both look alike!

Protect yourself – under "Settings", find "PRIMARY EMAIL" by your name, click on "Change". Add all of your email addresses (work and home).

If it's already happened, pick one account as "the best". Re-invite anyone not connected to it and copy and paste any profile text into it. After doing this, login to the bad account(s) go to "Settings" → "Account" and find the "Close your Account" link and follow those instructions. If that doesn't work out, or you no longer have access to the duplicate account, you'll need to contact LinkedIn support and ask them to remove the bad account(s). (and register all of your email addresses as above after they've been freed)

Action: Search for yourself on LinkedIn – take action if you have multiple accounts. Register all of your valid email addresses.

Do you see now how you can find, get found, and network your way to success with LinkedIn?

Wrapping Things Up

All training sessions start with a motivated student who has a goal: getting better at this task. The LinkedIn Personal Trainer creates a training environment for you every time you pick it up – you're the student, and the goal is to get more out of LinkedIn.

Find

Find based on what you're looking for, what's in other people's profiles, and who you connect to. The more precise your search, the more information others have in their profiles, and the larger your network - the better results you'll find.

Get Found

You get found based on what's in your profile and whom you connect to. The more information you have, and the larger network you are a part of - the more you'll get found.

and Network

Keep in touch and take small actions to stay connected to people you enjoyed being with. Build and maintain connections that will serve you for a lifetime. It's not what or who you know, or even who knows you, it's how well your network runs.

Your Way

By now you realize that there is no formula for success. Your life: your contacts, your activities, your skills and strengths – everything that makes you "you" – is unique. By understanding how LinkedIn works, you will be set to work with it in your own way.

To Success

It is out there, and my hope is that this guide puts you one step closer to reaching your goals in life. LinkedIn can help you along your way.

Have you checked out

www.linkedinpersonaltrainer.com?

Action:

Go and use LinkedIn!

If part of your success hinges on reaching as many people as possible, can you see why a large network full of weak connections might work for you?

Appendix A: Mega-Connectors

A product is successful when it is being used in ways that the original creators never intended. That happens with LinkedIn.

Throughout this guide, I have referred to *trusted contacts*, emphasizing that you will connect to, recommend, refer, match and otherwise work with your *trusted* contacts.

That model works very well, but is not the only model.

Some individuals believe that the best network is the largest network. They don't care about knowing the people they are connected to, just that they are connected.

This gives them a network that has an extensive reach – thousands of first level connections, millions of third level.

With this network, they are able to search extensively.

It comes with a downside though. When faced with a request to introduce people, recommend, or otherwise interact, they may not know either party. A forward reference through them is half-hearted or well-meaning at best, and does not assure either party that the other can be trusted. And given the extensive network that they have, they may well be inundated with requests – and unable to keep up.

It reminds me of the restrictions on the Genie in Disney's *Aladdin* – Phenomenal cosmic powers! Itty-bitty living space...

How quickly do you recognize

the capabilities of superheroes?

How quickly can a reader

recognize your capabilities?

Appendix B: Strategy Guide to Jumpstart Your Career with LinkedIn

The main portion of this book will help every user become more familiar with LinkedIn, but there's one aspect of the system that calls out for attention: employment. We want to take a look at the employment issue primarily from the job seeker's perspective, but also from the employer's perspective. When you understand both, you'll be more effective at using the system to manage your career.

Every experienced professional should be able to describe themselves through their profile, find and connect to past co-workers, use the system to find the "right" individual, and make introductions. Most will plan to continue on in their chosen career, but some will be breaking into a new career.

For those that plan a career shift, the system is just as valuable. By tapping into the otherwise hidden connections of your existing network, you'll be able to identify leads quickly and receive warm introductions – and get going much faster. If you're in this camp, read this section and constantly say to yourself: "Who else do the people I network with know? How can I leverage those relationships to help this new career?"

Part I: Profile

Your profile is the place to begin. Does it effectively position you within your field? If you were searching, would you want to take the time to talk to the person that appears to stand behind this profile? Do you stand apart from everyone else in a crowded profession? Your profile defines your brand.

Let's take a look at profile components.

How many professionals do you

meet over the course of a year?

Profile Components:

- Headline – the brand in one line
- Summary – the whole brand
- Specialties – niche capabilities that support the brand
- Job Descriptions – enhancing details
- Groups – professional involvement
- Other Information – social competence and stability

You will be defined by the impression that your profile makes on the reader. The question is: will this position you as someone that should be considered?

Be sure to include details that will bring your profile up for a specific skill search – remember, you won't be found for items you don't list.

Don't go overboard though; keep in mind the length of your profile and the information included. Consider editing information that might be better left out, and don't take 300 words to describe something that can be concisely portrayed in 80.

Part II: Connections

Some people seem to have the ability to build and maintain connections throughout their careers. Unfortunately, you may not be one of them – and this poses an issue.

LinkedIn makes it easy to re-connect with the people you've worked with over the years, maintain connections with people you know right now, and eases the effort to meet new people. With LinkedIn's searching capabilities, you'll want to re-establish connections with a wide variety of people that you've come across in both professional and personal activities.

Let's have a look at the people you should connect to.

*Do you search for the
person that will hire you?
The organization's HR manager?
Or Both?*

Places you've encountered people to connect with:

- Employers
- Professional organizations
- Neighborhood associations
- Religious affiliations
- Sports clubs
- School boosters
- Parent organizations
- Community associations…

The list is huge – you've been around, and should connect to the people you know and trust.

Once you've established this connection on LinkedIn, it is much less likely that you'll ever "lose" contact. As long as users keep information up-to-date, the system will maintain communication links.

Part III: Search

LinkedIn's advanced search functionality isn't difficult to use, but recognizing when to use it has been an issue.

For the job seeker, it's a perfect mechanism to research organizations, discover friends of friends with inside access, and perform background checks before interviews. The requirement is that as a searcher, you must be able to describe the kind of person that you'd like to find (within the boundaries of the search system).

LinkedIn is just as perfect for the recruiter. The recruiter can search based on job requirements and find candidates that have exactly those skills. They can contact the candidates at the top of the list and proceed with those that indicate the opening might be of interest.

Have you attempted an introduction through LinkedIn before you "needed" it to work?

Remember that employers can conduct background checks with friends of friends just as job searchers can.

After reviewing search strategies, it might be useful to reconsider the material you put in your profile. If you're searching for a job, can a potential employer find you, recognize the skills you bring to the table, and be interested enough to want to have a conversation? If you're looking to find a new employee, when a potential hire checks into your company and individual profiles on LinkedIn, are they still going to be interested in working for you?

Part IV: Introductions

The LinkedIn introduction represents the pot of gold at the end of the rainbow. With it, users can put all of these aspects together:

1. Construct an attractive profile that sets the brand.

2. Search through the millions of users within the LinkedIn database to find the "right" individual.

3. Find out who you know that knows them.

4. Arrange for a stellar introduction.

5. Remain available for situations when others search.

Useful when you're actively looking and useful when you aren't! This cycle of use is taking chunks out of job boards, and shows no indications of slowing down.

Many professionals stay away from job boards when they aren't actively looking. Because LinkedIn isn't just for landing a job, it's socially acceptable to build and maintain a presence on the site. (LinkedIn is just as useful for those attempting to be successful at a job, and that involves finding people for different reasons)

In this and everything else, I wish you continued success.

You'll find more than 300 articles covering additional topics and information about new features on LinkedInPersonalTrainer.com

Index

Subscribe via email or RSS on the

LinkedInPersonalTrainer.com website to

stay up to date and informed.

About the Author

Steve Tylock is a Problem Solver, Strategist, Creative Thinker, Author, Artist, Existential Outfitter, Husband, Father, and Child of God. He says so right on his LinkedIn profile:

http://www.linkedin.com/in/stevetylock

His professional experience includes supporting IT infrastructure from early system administration roles through team leadership, management, and overall technology direction. He has consulted in education, product development, manufacturing, government, small and large business environments.

His love of singing and community theater has put him on and off stage for a number of years; he is currently performing with the Traveling Cabaret. He has fun orienteering (running with a purpose) in the parks of Western New York, and has equal enjoyment skiing when snow is on the ground. Other interests include boating, hiking, fishing, golfing, and most any manner of game playing.

The youngest of six himself, Steve and his wife raise their four children in a suburban home that also includes various family pets and temporary guests of all sizes.

Follow @SteveTylock on twitter